# Cat Tales

**By Rosemary Byers**
**Cats by Alice Carroll**
**Edited By Robert Pace**

## Contents





Cover design by Barkat Curtin

2387

# Cat Nap

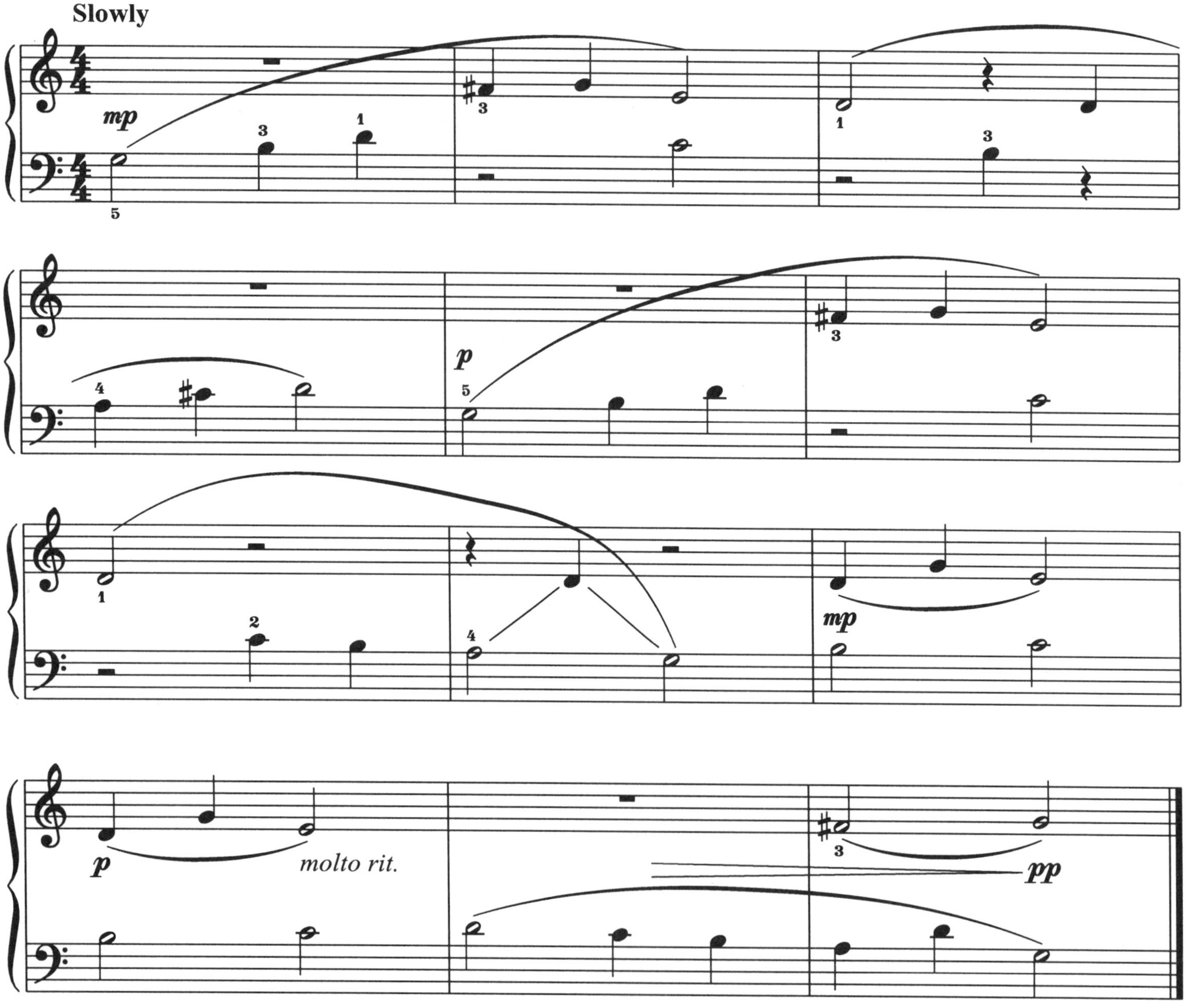

# Cat Fever

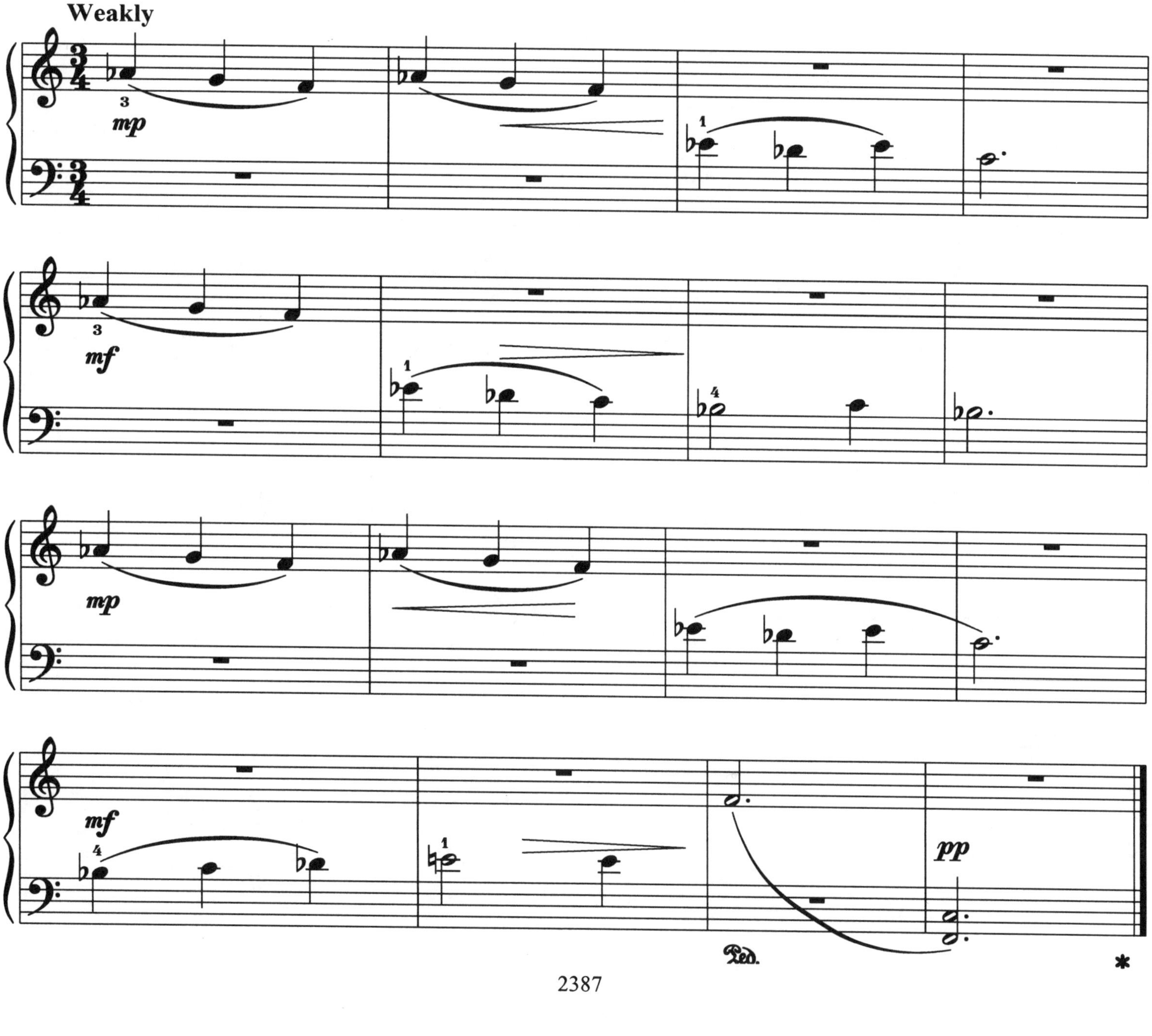

# Copy Cats

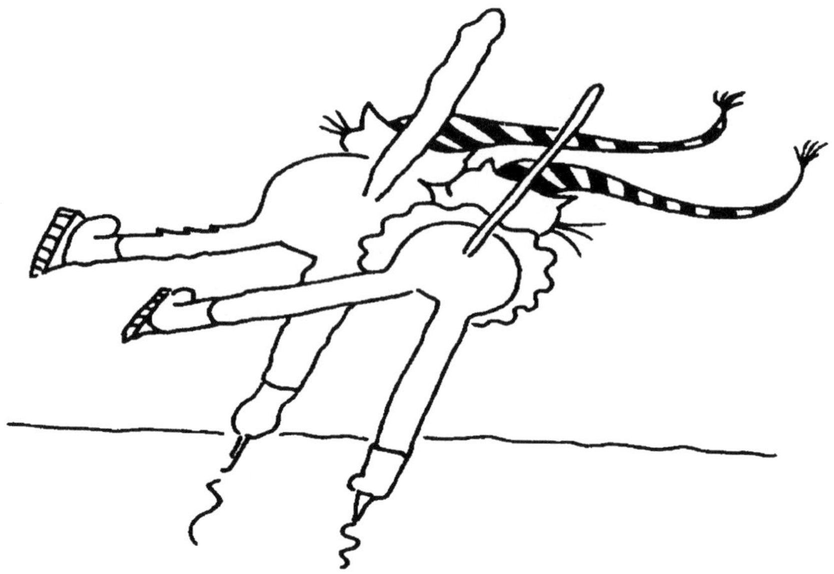

# Cat Pause

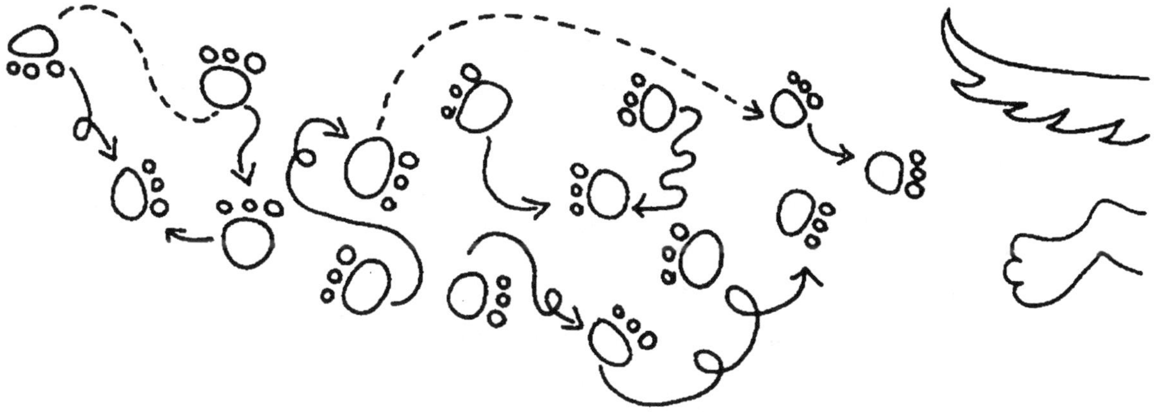

# Aristocats

**"Snobbishly" (and not too fast, ♩ = 126)**

# Cat Walk

# Kitty Cat Splat!

* Just grab a fistful of notes somewhere around those that are written. It's the effect that matters – not the specific notes!

** Play the real notes this time!

# Glamour Puss

# Cat Burglar

# Kitten on the Keys

Stems up = R.H.
Stems down = L.H.

# Catfish Ballet

Stems up = R.H.
Stems down = L.H.

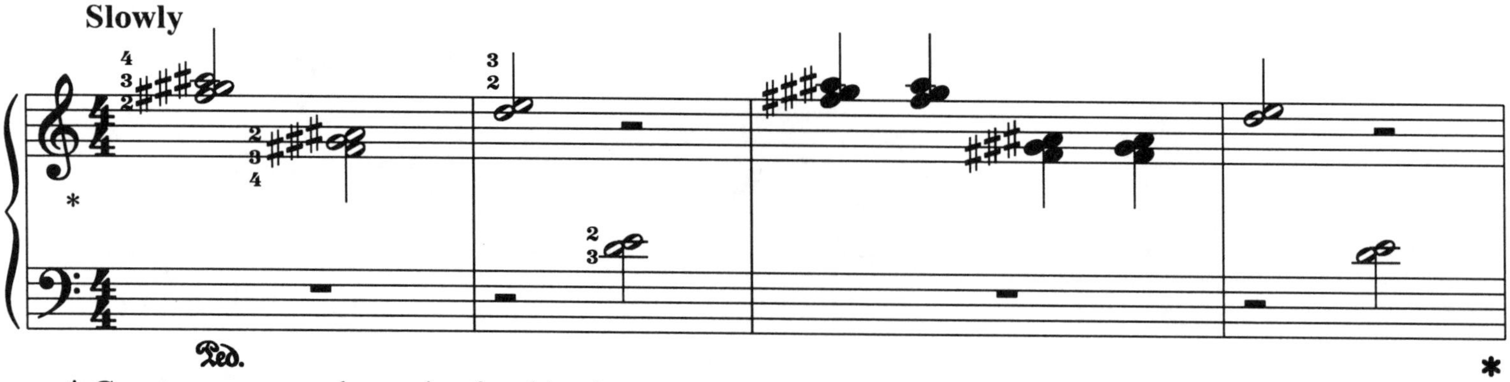


* Create your own dynamics for this piece.

Ped.
Ped.
Ped.
8va

# The Cat and the Canary

suddenly fast
f
molto ritardando

Singing
f
pp
molto rit.
ppp

# Midnight Meow